Why Your Customers Go Somewhere Else

Common Sense Ways to Ensure Your Service Department Customers Visit More, Spend More, and Defect Less

By

Randy Johnson

of Car People Marketing, Inc.

Published by Car People Marketing, Inc.
2650 N. Dixie Freeway
New Smyrna Beach, FL 32168
866-227-7337| www.carpeoplemarketing.com

ISBN: 978-0-9855228-0-3

Acknowledgements

*T*o my parents and grandparents, for raising me the right way, teaching me right from wrong, giving me a good work ethic, and for being there when I needed them.

To my wife, Kalyn, for her love, support, patience, and for everything she does so I can do what I love to do everyday.

To John May, my best friend since we were kids—my brother from another mother—for his friendship, sense of humor, and for the strength he gives me just by being my friend.

To Larry Hill, Dennis Higginbotham, Terry Taylor, and Gary Yeomans for their confidence in me, for giving me a chance, and for everything I've learned from them over the years.

To the entire team at Car People Marketing, especially Travis Whitaker, Terri Jones, Josh Hays, Marc Larabel, Tracy Griffith, and Dave Gopsill for doing what they all do so well.

To Wendy Scheuring and Mark Henderson for their amazing writing and editing skills and all of their help in putting this book together.

Table of Contents

Section I:
The Need for Change

Section II
How to Change: Where to Focus Your Resources

"Anything"

You can be anything, have anything, and do anything in this one-time, awesome opportunity called 'life' if you just consistently, persistently believe when others don't, stand up when others sit, love when others hate, give when others take, work when others quit, try when others give up, tell the truth when others lie, run when others walk, and succeed when others fail.

~~*Randy Johnson*

Foreword

I have always believed that everything happens for a good reason—that we are where we are at this very moment because of things that happened to us or things we did or didn't do in the past. I've also always believed that we are in control of 90% of the things that happen to us, good and bad. And I also believe that every day, we make choices—some important and some not—but choices nonetheless that can eventually affect our future.

Even when we get out of bed in the morning, we're faced with choices: Do I feel positive about the day ahead? Or, am I cranky? Am I going to let stuff bother me or am I going to shake it off and look on the bright side?

Similarly, businesses have choices. All businesses. As the winds of the economy bring change—and the economy is *always* changing—businesses have to adapt to these changes, or they will fall away. If they refuse to make adjustments, they will fail. It's just that plain and simple.

I also believe that in order to be good at anything, you have to love it. You have to have passion for it. Success without passion just goes against the grain. If you love what you do for a living, you will have a much better chance of succeeding—it just feels easier to reach your goals.

I've spent my career in the car business, and I absolutely love what I do! The biggest kick I get every day is helping other people in the car business succeed! I don't believe in mediocrity, and I don't believe in maintaining the status quo. I have always said that if you expect to survive and succeed, you have to keep pumping—just like riding a bike. If you decide to just coast and you stop pedaling, you will eventually coast to a stop. So don't stop pumping— coasting sucks, and stopping sucks even more!

I feel like my job is to help you realize your true potential and grow your business beyond what you might think you can. I want you to thrive when everyone else may tell you that it's simply impossible—just like I did when everyone told me what I wanted to do wasn't possible. And that's why I feel driven to write this book!

This book is divided into two sections: 1) The Need for Change—Why the "old way" doesn't work anymore; and 2) How to Change—Where to focus your resources. Throughout the book, you'll find "Common Sense Service Tips" that you'll want to remember, so they're easily identified for quick reference. (They're also listed in Appendix A.)

I hope that you will find this book easy to read, and I hope it will even entertain you a little bit; but most importantly, I hope it will motivate you to reach new heights in your business that you've never imagined!

~~Randy Johnson

~~Section I~~

The Need for Change

~~Chapter 1~~

If You Always Do What You Always Did

We've all heard people say that you have to have vision in order to succeed in business, to anticipate trends of the future before they happen. All those young business people who have made millions because of Internet-based businesses are proof of that. But I also think there is another type of vision that's overlooked:

re-vision—seeing what's already there but looking at it in a different light.

Let me explain.

I have been in the auto service business all of my life. I love it. Because of the line of work that I am in, I talk to a lot of dealers. But I remember one dealer in particular, and you'll soon see why he is so memorable. When I started to broach the subject of the 2008 economic downturn with him, he questioned me: "What are you talking about? What recession? I've done the best business that I ever have in this so-called downturn." He told me how and why he was enjoying record car sales, record service sales, and record profits. He told me he had always been focused on customer retention, and while he admitted that the economy did cause him some worry, that just made him focus more on his customers, more on his employees, and more on his service department than he ever had before. He didn't stop managing, he managed more. He didn't stop selling, he sold even more. And he didn't stop advertising, he advertised even more.

He said service advertising was a big pay-off because not only did he keep his clientele, he actually *increased* his business while many other dealerships were folding. The lesson I learned from him was a simple one that everybody has heard before, but one that's sometimes forgotten: If things get tough, you need to step it up a notch and work even harder! You know, 'when the going gets tough, the tough get going.'

I always find it fascinating how our perceptions shape what we consider to be reality. For example, around the same time period, I had another similar discussion with yet another dealer; but this time, I got a completely different reaction:

"I'm so glad that I no longer have to go through *that* again," he said to me.

"That?"

"Yeah," he added with kind of a smug look on his face. "You know, having to get involved in the service department. I just want to get back to business as usual, the business of selling cars again. I don't like it back there."

"What? Back *there*? Didn't you learn anything?" I wanted to punch him in the face. It was like he had done his time— served his prison sentence—and now that he was out of jail, he felt as if he could go back to the sexy world of selling cars again and forget about service! *Back there* was what kept him in business so he could still be here! Idiot.

I really thought that he might have figured out that his service and parts departments were profit centers that deserved as much attention and focus as the sales department. I mean, they did keep his store in business over the past few years. You would think he wouldn't forget that, right? I also thought that he had figured out that customer retention and service traffic—and cool stuff like effective labor rates, dollars per repair order, and productivity—were as important and just as 'sexy' as selling cars; but, as the Blue Collar comic, Ron White would say, "I was wrong!" He didn't get it, but like I said earlier, it's all in how you perceive it. It's all in the vision. What many dealerships don't recognize is that *service is important*—no, *critical*—to the success of the dealership.

You might be thinking that in theory this all sounds good, but how can we make it a reality? If we perceive it that way, will it just happen? No, we have to *will* it that way. We have to realize that we need to change the way we think about service. We have to know why we need to change and how we need to change before we can start along the journey of change. That makes sense, right? And, we need to view change as a challenge, as fun, and not as drudgery. That is how you will make change happen.

Here is an example: For as long as I can remember, dealers have spent thousands and thousands of dollars on car sales advertising, but they spent as little as they possibly could on service advertising. What were they thinking? What *are* they thinking? Don't let your service department be the best kept secret in town. Get the word out! Advertise. Change. Succeed.

My ex-boss, Larry Hill, use to say, "If you always do what you always did, you will always get what you always got." And I like to add to that, "If you are lucky, you will always get what you always got."

To quote the old *Hill Street Blues* line, "It's a jungle out there." The rule of the "jungle" is that only the fittest survive. So, do you have the vision and the will to make your service business survive, thrive, and prosper? I hope you do. And the good news is, it isn't that difficult. It isn't rocket science, guys!

~~Chapter 2~~

The Missing Link

We've all heard the term, "the missing link." For decades, scientists have searched and searched for "the missing link." And yet, they still haven't found it. However, when it comes to car dealerships, I can say that there is also a "missing link"; but, it's not waiting to be discovered, it's just waiting to be realized. For years, the importance of this link has just plain been ignored. Wake up, guys! Understanding what the missing link is and working toward strengthening that link is vital to the bread and butter of your dealership. So what's the secret? Actually, when it comes to car dealerships, the "missing link" is not much of a secret at all!

Throughout my interactions with car dealers and observations of how dealerships are run, I realized that there has always been a link between car sales and car service. But more often than not, dealerships have failed to recognize that car sales and car service go hand in hand. Good sales will provide increased service opportunities, and in turn, good service experiences will provide brand and dealership loyalty resulting in increased car sales.

Later on, I'll explain in detail what I think it takes to make a service department great, but let me just say now that the vehicle sales department folks need to understand more about service, and the service guys need to understand more about sales. It should be the goal of the sales team as well as the service team to get every car buyer into the dealership's service department, and not only that, to keep them coming back!

Common Sense Service Tip #1:

Once a month, get service and sales people together for a short 30-minute meeting to discuss the importance of working together. Invite service advisors to a vehicle sales meeting, and invite sales managers and sales people to a service meeting. It's good to know what the other guys are doing, to walk in the other man's shoes, you know.

The key is to recognize that new and used car sales are joined at the hip with car service. When you recognize the importance of this relationship, you will begin to change the culture of your organization—to create a culture of *interdependence*, where everybody realizes that the health of the team is dependent upon everyone on that team. Then real growth and sustainable success will follow!

Chapter 3

Creating a Culture of Interdependence

As we mentioned in the previous chapter, it is critical to the profitability and the very survival of the dealership to move from every department doing its own thing to everybody being dependent upon one another for their success. To do this, the management team needs to change the culture; it must create a culture of *interdependence*.

As you've probably heard, established organizations often resist change. I think that is due in part to the way changes are ushered in and then implemented, and also because people have experienced initiatives that petered out after the "rah-rah" and gnashing of teeth were over. I've watched various "fads" come and go, often times with little positive effect on the bottom line.

But interdependence is not a fad. Rather, it is an essential building block to long-term profitability. So, the question is: How *do* you change the culture of your organization?

For starters, the entire management team from the top down needs to understand and appreciate the value of every single player on your team. One of the great attributes of the late great football coach, Vince Lombardi, was that he possessed an intrinsic and genuine respect for his fellow man, including *everybody* in his organization, from the water boy to the quarterback. Every single person in the organization felt valued and then did whatever he could to help the team succeed. The Lombardi Green Bay Packers organization showed how interdependence resulted in a successful organization!

But most of you are not playing football. You're in the automotive industry—new car sales, used car sales, automotive service, parts or collision centers, managing one or more of these activities, or perhaps even supporting them. Do you value and appreciate everybody on your team? Really value and appreciate? And I'm not talking personalities here. Every organization has somebody who just thinks differently or who does things differently than you do. Heck, I have some of those in my own company! But regardless of our *very different* opinions, I still absolutely value and appreciate what they contribute to the team.

I think it's primarily up to the management team of any automotive business to create this culture of interdependence, although everybody from your service advisors to your newest shop techs to your top sales people need to play, too, for this culture to really take root. So, let me say a little something to the people in some of the major roles of the car business:

Dealer Principals and General Managers: You need to get your sales, service, and parts departments playing on the same team. It's up to you to break down the traditional walls that exist between them. You have to meet with people and show them how their success (and the success of the dealership) is dependent on "those other guys." Service needs sales; sales needs service; service needs parts; parts needs service. They all need each other to make this thing work. It's that simple. And you can't just talk the talk—you *have* to walk the walk and lead by example. You spiff your sales people, so why not spiff your service people? You set goals for sales; you need to do the same for service and you need to start running your service department like it was a sales department, because frankly, it is.

Your store probably has weekly or even daily sales meetings for your vehicle sales people to train, motivate and set goals right? So why don't you have service sales meetings to do the same thing for your service team? They need to be trained and motivated and they need to know what you expect just as much, if not more, than your vehicle sales people. You need to hold your service team accountable for reaching their goals and you need to praise them when they do well, and you need to bust on them a little bit when they get off course. They need to know that you know what is going on in your store.

Common Sense Service Tip #2:

It's common practice to take out the sales team or key salespeople to a nice dinner when they achieve or exceed a sales goal. It is not nearly as common to take out service advisors and even less common to take out the service techs (except for maybe the holiday dinner). Fix this. Fix this now! A few cold pizzas just won't cut it, guys!

Also, you need to get your vehicle sales people learning from the service department. Service guys know stuff that can help the sales people sell cars, you know. And, I bet your service sales manager(s), among others, might be able to learn some good sales techniques and improve their selling skills from your sales people. Develop training to be taught by one group to the other, and then flip it.

Service Managers: You need sales! Trust me. They sell cars that burn gas and bring you work. They can also help you improve your own sales skills—overcoming objections, creating win-win situations for every potential customer, and the list goes on. And let's face it, the smarter those guys on the sales floor are about the vehicles they're selling and you're servicing—not to mention the services you offer in your shop—the more service work they're going to bring you. Get your techs and advisors to take time out to educate their teammates in the sales department. And please sensitize your techs not to speak techno-mumbo-jumbo to their teammates in sales! They may or may not know the difference between a ratchet and a screwdriver, so have your guys speak in a language the other guys can understand—and don't forget to reward those who do.

Sales Managers: You need service! Trust me. They can do more to create brand

and dealership loyalty—and therefore, more returning customers—than you can imagine. The old line that "sales" sells the first car and "service" sells the rest is still very true today. Think about it. Satisfied, loyal service customers are much more likely to buy their next car *where* they get that one serviced. And whenever they're in your dealership for service, it's easier for them to browse around your lot and check out your newer models, planting that seed for when they need or want another vehicle or recommending you to their friends.

Service people can also educate your sales force about maintenance requirements, accessory operation, how to adjust the clock, and what to do when something goes wrong—in other words, everything from what makes 'em great to what makes 'em go to how to keep 'em going. Go visit your teammates in the service shop, and start rotating your sales people through the shop during the slow times. They can learn *a lot* about the vehicles you're trying to sell. And if you've been selling cars for more than a week, you know you have potential customers who come in who have "nuts & bolts" questions about your cars. They want to know why this feature was designed, how much horsepower, how often to change out this filter, or how this techno-widget really improves performance. If your salespeople don't know—or worse, they try to fake it— more often than not, there goes a potential sale. Have your sales people talk to your service techs and service advisors. If your sales people don't understand, ask your techs to re-explain.

Conclusion: If everybody from the top dog in the dealership to the newest tech or salesperson will start implementing these common sense improvements, a culture of interdependence will begin to take root. There will be increased employee satisfaction, which will result in increased customer satisfaction. This will in turn result in increased customers to the car sales and service sales departments, which will naturally result in improved profitability for the entire dealership team. Everybody wins.

Chapter 4

The Competition Is Pigging Out: And You ARE on the Menu!

*O*n your way to work tomorrow, I want you to count the number of places where you can have your car serviced. There are multiple tire chains, brake specialists, quick-lube specialists, independent and chain garages capable of overhauling, fixing, or replacing everything that's between the bumpers, including the bumpers. And know this: Your customers are driving past those same stores every day, too! Those automotive service businesses are just like you, competing for those same customers—your service customers! Remember, your biggest service competitors are not the local dealerships; your main competitors are the independent service shops in your area.

Now, when you get to your store, start thinking like a customer: Go online and Google terms like "auto repair" or "tires" or "oil change" and check out how many flashy, enticing websites pop up. With your customer glasses on, ask yourself: Where would *I* call or visit if I were a real customer? And if you really want to know more about who your competition is, find out who your top 10 wholesale parts customers are. These guys are buying parts from you so that they can install them on the cars that belong to the customers they stole from you—your service customers! Think about that for just a moment: Your wholesale parts customers are servicing the cars that used to come to *your* store. I don't know how you feel about that, but man, that just kills me.

You have to know this: Your competitors aren't stupid; they are very sharp. They advertise well; they locate well; they price well. They compete, and they fully understand that it's a win or die struggle, every day. They are fighting for your customers and quite frankly, many of you guys are just letting them win.

I am convinced that had we done our collective job right from the get-go, there would not be nearly the swarm of auto service competitors out there that there is today. But the fact is that we did not; we did not get convenient. We did not get competitive. We did not focus on customer pay service, customer satisfaction, or customer retention. Oops! Shame on all of us—but, it's not too late.

Now think about this: Every single car on the road, in a parking lot or even in a salvage yard, started out as a brand new car that was purchased from a dealership. At that time, we had 100% customer retention and we just let all of those customers slip through our fingers and go to the competition. Now, regardless of how or why we let that happen, it happened. Entrepreneurs recognized the market need and began to capitalize. Maybe slowly at first, but more and more, they began to eat our lunch. Now, they are pigging out, and guess what? You ARE on the menu. In fact, you are the Special of the Day!

To compound the drop-off in dealership service customers, warranty work declined, mandatory service intervals were stretched, and cars were built better and just don't break as often as they used to. But perhaps the most costly effect of the shift from dealership service to non-dealerships was that the important customer relationship cycle—the relationship that should start in the sales department that carries over to the service department and back to vehicle sales over the lifetime ownership of a car—was broken. This is the crux of the double-whammy that has many dealerships on the ropes.

Now, before you slit your wrists and think about giving up, look at this as a challenge and an opportunity. I hope you get serious. I hope you get mad. In fact, I hope you get really mad—mad enough to want to kick some tail—mad enough to be willing and ready to roll up your sleeves to go to war with the competition. Beat them at the game they started and make them wish they had never gotten into the game in the first place. Whew!

Some of you might remember the middleweight boxer, "Marvelous Marvin" Haggler. He was known for his gentleman nature...*outside* of the boxing ring. But in the ring, he was a relentless warrior. Once a reporter asked him about this stark contrast; how he could change from being such a nice guy to such an intense fighter the minute he stepped through the ropes. I'll never forget his answer.

In response, he squinted his eyes, his lips snarled, and his whole demeanor took on a genuine intensity when he said, "When I get into the ring, I look across at that other guy and think, 'He's trying to steal food out of my little baby's mouth,' because he is. And I will die fighting like an animal to keep someone from taking *my* baby's food!" Watching this on TV, I knew—absolutely knew—he was dead serious.

I think we all need to take a page out of the "Marvelous Marvin" philosophy playbook for success. We need to approach turning around our service business as if "the other guys" are trying to take the food from our babies' mouths, because they are. We need to light that fire in our own bellies to strive for success, to train with intensity and to fight with a renewed passion to bring customers back to our service departments where they belong.

~~Chapter 5~~

Dealership: Another Dirty Word?

I've said it before and I'll say it again: I really love what I do. Not a lot of people can honestly say that they *love* going to work every single day. But to tell you the truth, I haven't been "to work" in years. I get up every morning and go to "fun."

Yes, I really do love the car business. I love the excitement, the enthusiasm, the creativity and the energy, and I love the people that are in it.

I knew I loved cars and was some day going to be in the car business way back when I was an eight-year-old boy growing up in the hills of West Virginia. My dad worked on cars all the time, and I spent most of my nights and Saturdays watching and learning from him. In fact, throughout my teenage years, I fixed cars—old cars that seemed to most to be beyond repair. I felt it was an art (and a lot of fun) to take a car headed for the junkyard and make its engine purr and its paint shine again, and in some cases make it better than when it had rolled off of the factory floors.

You must also love the automobile industry or you wouldn't be in it and you probably wouldn't be reading this book. And if you are a service manager, I truly believe that you have *the most* important mission at your dealership: To re-invent your potential customers' view of what the words "dealership" and "dealership service" mean. My question to you is, "Are you ready to take on that responsibility?"

To illustrate a little better, let's play a word game. Let's take the word "mother-in-law." No, not *your* mother-in-law specifically, just the word "mother-in-law". (Just for the record, I love *my* mother-in-law. But that's not the point!) Write a list of as many associations you can with the word "mother-in-law". Now, what kinds of associations did you come up with? Did you write down "nagging", "mean-spirited", "interfering"," difficult", or other words that may be even more negative? Now, remember, that doesn't mean that *your* mother-in-law is any of those things; it's just that the word "mother-in-law" carries a lot of negative associations for most people.

Don't believe me? Then think about this. Say there is an older lady in your life—a neighbor or dear friend—to whom you would like to send a greeting card. Now answer this question: Would you rather buy her a greeting card that says, "You're like a mother to me," or "You're like a mother-in-law to me"? Which greeting card would be the compliment and which one would be the insult? I think you're starting to get my point.

Now you may be thinking: What does this word game have to do with me or the dealership? Well, what associations do people make with the word "dealership"? Think about it. If you can't come up with an answer on your own, try asking your non-dealership friends to make a list for you. I bet you'll find words like "expensive", "inefficient", "unhelpful", "slow", "bad customer service", "dirty restrooms", "dimly-lit waiting rooms with a flickering TV that plays soap operas", and more. Trust me, the list of negative associations many people have with car dealerships and dealership service goes on and on.

So, as a manager, you do have a challenging job. And you also have one of the most important missions in the industry: to re-create what the words "dealership service" mean to most people. It's up to you to take the "dirty" out of the word "dealership," and replace it with the word "deal". And you also have to put the "service" back in service—and you can start with your own shop. Remember that song, "Let there be peace on earth and let it begin with me?" Well, let there be a "deal" in dealership, and let it begin with me. It's up to you to make your customers your priority, and to make your dealership a place where people *want* to come.

Chapter 6

Does *Your* Service Department Scare People Away?

*I*t started out as just a normal morning. Sure, I had places to be, but I had to make a quick stop to buy a cup of coffee because I wasn't quite awake yet. I hopped back into the car and it wouldn't start. *Great.* I hit the ignition again. *Nothing.* So I asked someone for a jump and tried it again, and still not even a click! Like I said, I had places to go, people to see, but my car wasn't cooperating. I figured I would call the dealership since I had been a pretty loyal customer. Surely, they'd help me in a fix, I thought. After all, I had already bought five cars from them.

When I called the dealer, it took what seemed like forever to get through to the service department after being transferred a couple or more times, being put on what I call "terminal hold" and actually being accidently hung up on once. It's ok. I am in this business. I understand. I will just call back again—and I did (even though most normal people wouldn't have.)

Eventually, a Service Advisor picked up the phone and answered in a loud, rushed voice: "Service." I explained my predicament, and that I needed to get my car towed to their shop. What I heard on the other end of the phone just blew me away and I bet it will blow you away too.

"Okay," the Service Advisor said matter-of-factly. "Call a wrecker and get it down here."

I swore under my breath. I didn't believe or want to believe what I had just heard. But that's exactly what he said. There was no compassion in his voice. No empathy. No inquiring questions. Just the clipped phrase: "Call a wrecker." What a moron!

"Well, I don't know who to call," I tried to explain before he cut me off and rattled off a phone number for a wrecker service so fast that a court reporter would have messed up the number, and then he quickly told me to have a good day and hung up. He hung up! He hung up!

Common Sense Service Tip #3:

Whenever a customer calls your shop and is broken down, please, for Pete's sake, make sure your service advisors know that they need to take control, take action and call the tow truck for the customer. It's called "customer service" for a reason, and a customer that is broken down needs help. This is an opportunity for your service department to shine—to be that help to a desperate customer in need, when they need it most.

"Have a good day," he said. Well, I can tell you that I was *not* having a good day, so I decided to call the local Firestone store that was just a few blocks away. I had been there on two other occasions—Saturday afternoon once and a Sunday morning, when my dealer service department was closed—and for the record, as crazy as this may sound, both experiences there were exceptional!

A guy named Jordan politely answered, and after he heard my story, he said, "Oh, I am sorry you are having trouble. Are you in any immediate danger? Is your vehicle off on the side of the road? Did you try to jump it? Did it make a noise? Are the lights dim or bright? Don't worry; I will handle this for you." Wow!

I could hardly believe my ears as Jordan continued. "Let's do this: Give me your address and phone number, and I will have a wrecker company come right over and get you and the car. They will call you in a few minutes for directions and to let you know that they are on their way, if that's OK, and we will get the car here, diagnose what's wrong and get you a quote. It's probably just the battery, and unfortunately, we don't stock the battery for your car so I will get one on its way from our warehouse, so that way we can speed up the process when you get here, ok?" OK? OK? How about wow—again!

I was awestruck by that phone conversation. I was amazed by Jordan's professionalism. That guy had completely turned my day around and he worked at the local independent Firestone store! Again, wow!

Within ten minutes, the towing company called me and, after a few more minutes, the tow truck had arrived and my car was loaded onto the wrecker. But then, I suddenly remembered that my battery was still under warranty from the dealership. No matter how nice and accommodating Jordan was, there was no way I was going to pay for a battery when I could get it replaced for free under warranty. So I had the tow truck take me and my car to a different dealership—other than the one I had called earlier—on the other side of town.

When we got to that dealership, the service advisor there told me (much to my surprise!) that my battery was actually *out of warranty* because the original battery had already been replaced. It turns out that the warranty for the replacement was already expired. The end result? If I wanted a new battery (my friggin' third battery), I was going to have to pay for it. Who could've figured that one out? (Maybe they have a problem with batteries, ya think?) So, I ended up shelling out $236.00 for a battery that I just knew would have been cheaper at Firestone! My day was going from good to bad again. It's a good thing my phone rang just then because I could think of a few choice words to say to that service advisor.

I answered the phone and it was Jordan. Jordan? Crap, I forgot about Jordan from Firestone. His call took me by surprise. "Mr. Johnson, I'm just calling to see if you are alright. You hadn't arrived with the tow truck and so I just wanted to see if it ever arrived and if you're all right. We have your battery right here waiting on you." Jordan was accommodating, attentive, aggressive, and not only that, he was genuinely concerned.

I can't begin to tell you how badly I felt. In retrospect, I realized I should have called Jordan about the change in plans, so I apologized to him; but to be honest, I hadn't expected anyone to care that much. Nonetheless, I will say that Jordan went the extra mile to win my loyalty as a customer. And being no dummy, he probably knows that I have family and friends, all of whom I will tell about Firestone's over-the top customer service. Hey, I just told you about it! Oh, and in case you were wondering, I did ask Jordon how much the battery would have cost had it been installed at his place: $89. Isn't that special?

Common Sense Service Tip #4:

Show customers you care by calling when they miss an appointment. It will give you a chance to get them in again. Or, at the very least, you will

find out what happened to them or
why they went somewhere else.

So now you have to ask yourself some
hard questions: How many times have you
or your people turned a customer away?
How many customers won't come back to
your service department because of the lack
of service, or lack of simple, common sense
manners for that matter? Does your service
department scare people away?

~~Chapter 7~~

Why They Hate Us:
'The Big Bad 5'

*H*ave you wondered why your service drives aren't as busy as they should be? Have you just accepted that there are slow periods and that there is nothing you can do about it? How about your sales lot or showroom? Some might chalk it up to a stale economy. Others might be tempted to hope for a return of increased warranty work from the car manufacturers. But the reality is that no amount of blaming or wishful thinking is going to increase your business. What we have to do in any business is to make honest assessments of what's wrong and how we can fix it, and then we need to do something about it.

Years ago, I started to suspect that we in the dealership service business were doing something (or some things) to annoy and drive customers away…that is, away from our dealership service and right to the competition. But, I needed proof. As Gene Kranz—the NASA manager made popular in the movie, *Apollo 13*—said: "In God we trust. Everybody else bring data."

So I wanted data to see what, if anything, dealership service departments were doing to alienate customers and I wanted it to be real. I figured a great way to gather data was to conduct customer surveys. So, we surveyed more than 100 people and asked them what they hated most about dealership service departments. We told them to not hold back—to tell us how they really felt—and boy, did they. What was interesting was that the same five concerns or dislikes kept popping up. I admit that I figured these were a problem, but what surprised me was the order of the things they hated most. Whoa! Now that was an eye-opener.

Here are the "Top 5" things that tick people off about dealership service departments:

Reason #1. "Dealerships are not open when I need them to be open."

This is so simple; I'm almost too embarrassed to say it: How much money does your service shop make when you are closed? Nothing! Your competitors are open before and after work hours, on Saturdays, and sometimes even Sundays! They are making themselves more *convenient* to *your* potential customers!

Common Sense Service Tip #5:

Be open more! Expand the times you're open for business. Staff up so you have enough people to be open, give better service, and maintain a happy workforce, which, by the way, ensures great customer service. Try being open 7 to 7. Or here's a crazy idea: Have your service department open when the rest of the dealership is open—that will throw everyone a curve ball.

I think it is just nonsense that some departments close at different times in the same store. You are either open or not open; you can't be half open. It's like trying to be a little bit pregnant—it just doesn't work that way. Some retail stores do this, too; they close the pharmacy or the lawn and garden section long before the store closes. I wonder whose brilliant "bean counter" idea that was? Hey, you have to be open. You *have* to be convenient. It's just the way of the world nowadays. The days of "banker hours" are over. Heck, even bankers caught onto this one!

Maybe you really are open enough but your customers don't know it. They don't know your hours so they assume you are not open. Make sure they know that you are convenient. Advertise your hours boldly, and everywhere.

Common Sense Service Tip #6:

Another great idea that doesn't cost a dime, is stapling a small brochure to each repair order that tells customers all of the great reasons they should always use your store—especially your hours.

Reason #2. "I hate to call the dealership. They put me on hold, bounce me around, and oftentimes hang up on me!"

Customers tell us that they actually hate to call service departments. They *hate* it. You spend thousands of dollars each month to get customers to call and the way most dealers handle the phone is just horrible. People tell us they hate automated phone menus; they hate it when the phone rings off the wall; and, they hate it when they are put on hold forever or are sent to voicemail.

Common Sense Service Tip #7:

Get rid of phone systems that piss customers off. Kill automated phone menus. Kill phone banks. Kill voicemail. Hire enough service advisors to man your phones. If someone calls—and the data shows they usually do before bringing their car in for service—they are a potential customer. Show them you care; answer the phone, invite them in and close the deal.

Reason #3. "Dealerships are just not competitive on their pricing!"

Note that they didn't just say they wanted you to be the "cheapest"—they said be more *competitive!* You must compete on price for common services like oil changes, tire rotation, and tires, to name a few. Once you do, you can then sell the customer on your world class service. (Think Features, Benefits, Advantages, or "FBA".) You have to give customers reasons to do business with you. When you take the time to explain those reasons, you build value and the cost becomes less important, so you will be *more competitive* and improve the customer's perception. You have increased your perceived value to the customer!

Reason #4. "I dread having to go to the dealership for any service—even warranty work—because it takes them forever!"

Be faster. Get the right people, processes and equipment in place to service your customers' cars quickly. Every service manager should be managing turnaround times and productivity. Make guarantees you can keep, like "Oil changes in 30 minutes or less." Seriously, this is a no-brainer if you want to get customers back into your drives.

Common Sense Service Tip #8:

Have a rock solid express service process in place to get customers in, do the job right, inspect the car, and get them out in 30 to 45 minutes. Convenience is the key factor today. We live in a fast-paced, 24/7/365 world, and customers just will not go where they feel like they are wasting time.

Reason #5. "I think my dealership should remind me when my car is due for service, send me coupons and reward me for my patronage. I want to

be valued as a person at the place I choose to do business."

In addition to fantastic customer service—from birth-to-death, so to speak—make sure you consistently send money-saving service coupons and reminders to your customers. You have to keep your name in lights. And customers told us that they think dealers should remind them just like their doctor or dentist does. That makes sense! You should also consider implementing a rewards program for your customers. Almost every business has one and consumers are actually saying that they expect you to have one, too. Include real incentives to bring them back—service discounts of real value—and make sure your marketing programs include appointment reminders for members via email or even by phone.

Now that you have data to show why customers "hate" dealership service—and why they may not be choosing you to service their cars—it's up to you to change their minds. Start winning back your customers from the competition! The chapters in the next section of the book will go into more detail about the changes you should be making to get rid of the "big, bad 5."

~~Section II~~

How to Change:

Where to Focus Your Resources

~~Chapter 8~~

A Self-Assessment: Would You Do Business With You?

When you get up in the morning, do you look in the mirror to make sure you're walking out the door looking tip-top? I think most everybody does. You probably have a standard checklist you go through—whether or not you do it consciously or subconsciously—checking hair, face, clothes. When we do this, believe it or not, we're doing a quality assurance (QA) self-assessment, or audit. We're making sure that everything we did to get ready was done right—that we're not wearing socks that don't match, or we didn't miss a spot shaving, or whatever. Basically, we're just doing a self-check, or a QA audit.

Now let me dare you to do the same with your service department. You need to give yourself an honest, thorough self-assessment or QA audit. But first, you need to take off your manager hat and put on your customer hat. In other words, you need to think like a customer. Your mission is to get a totally honest answer to the question: *Would you do business with you?*

To get an even better assessment, enlist friends or acquaintances to be "mystery shoppers" and "ghost callers." Just like when we're looking in the mirror, sometimes we ask others to help: Does this match? Did I miss a spot on my neck? Etcetera.

Here are some easy, common sense things you can do to make your dealership service department look and feel like a first-class operation. Start by calling your shop and pretending to be a customer:

- How long does it take someone to answer the phone?
- When you call, does the service advisor introduce himself, and politely ask for your name and say, "How may I assist you today?"

- Does the service advisor take an interest in your problem and express genuine concern?
- Does the service advisor explain the features, benefits, and advantages of bringing your car in for service at your shop or does he just blurt out a price and hang up?
- Does the service advisor "close the deal" by asking when you would like to bring the car in by setting an appointment?

To get a customer's perspective of your dealership, ask your non-dealership friends or acquaintances to critique your shop by answering the following questions:

- Is the service department easy to find? Are there easy-to-follow signs and painted lanes directing you where to go for service?
- Does the facility look clean and inviting?
- Would you feel safe letting your loved ones come here alone?
- Are service advisors and techs standing around smoking and joking, waiting for

customers like vultures? Or are they engaged in their work?

- Are the service advisors and techs friendly and welcoming, or do they make you feel like you are interrupting them?
- How would you rate the employees' appearance? Are their uniforms clean and crisp? Is their hygiene impeccable?
- Is the intercom continually blaring?
- Does the service write-up counter look clean and professional or is it cluttered and disorganized?

Remember how I issued a dare at the beginning of this chapter? I *dared* you to engage in a thorough and honest self-assessment of your business just like you check yourself before leaving your house for work or an important engagement. If you have the nerve to take the dare, then you'll have the nerve to dig for the brutally honest answers required to improve.

And I dare you to do your research *before* you spend thousands of dollars in service advertising. Advertising may bring in more customers, but, as the old country saying goes, you don't want to write a check you can't cash. In other words, if you have pissing off customers down to a science, don't advertise to try to bring any more in until you "fix what's broken"—that's just dumb.

Once you're convinced that "Absolutely, yes!" is the answer to the question, "Would you do business with you?"—once your service department is a place that your customers will brag about—then it's time to advertise and crank up the volume.

~~Chapter 9~~

First Impressions Last Forever

I believe people form their first impressions of someone new within two minutes of their first meeting based on looks, dress, hygiene, body language, etc. And, I'd say that's pretty much how long you have to make or break your customers' first impressions of your service department.

If you want your sales and service departments to flourish, if you want to grow and sustain the success of your dealership, as I already said in the previous chapter, start by asking yourself the questions, "What first impression do *we* make on our customers?" and "When they first meet us, what do they see and think?"

When your customers drive up, what do they see? Do your shop and service drive look clean and professional? Is someone hurrying over to greet them warmly, to welcome them to your shop, and to let them know where to go or are they ignored or herded in like cattle?

When your customers walk up to your write-up area, what is the first thing they see? Who is the first person they talk to? Are they again greeted promptly in a polite and friendly way? Or do they have to wait a long time to finally get someone to acknowledge them?

What do customers see when they walk into your waiting room? Do they walk into a dirty, dingy room with a T.V. blaring a show they don't want to see? Or do they walk into a warm, comfortable, inviting place—a place where they can park themselves and pull out a good book or a laptop or smart phone? See if it is a place where you would want your wife and kids to hang out. Is it warm and inviting, or is it obnoxious? If you wouldn't want to sit in there, what makes you think that other people would?

I'm not saying that you have to have upscale furniture and fancy décor that you cannot afford, but you need to make your waiting room a comfortable place to sit, and a place where time won't seem to last forever. Be hospitable; think of your customer as your guest and find ways to offer "customer delight," such as clean floors, clean, comfortable chairs, clean drinking water and fresh coffee, and clean restrooms, stocked with soap, toilet paper, paper towels or a hand-dryer that works.

Did you notice I mentioned the word "clean" four times? Have Mr. Clean regularly sweep through your waiting room and restrooms. This is so important that you might even take 30 seconds and make a quick, daily swing through your facilities yourself. Remember the saying, cleanliness is next to Godliness? Make your customers feel as if they are in "dealership heaven" when they wait in your waiting room! Remember this adage: Clean and profit go hand-in-hand.

Common Sense Service Tip #9:

Make your waiting area a customer "wow" place. Offer free Wi-Fi, loaner IPads, or even a couple of arcade machines. Play games, show movies, have good books on-hand, or maybe include customer conveniences, like free manicures. Make customers *want* to visit your store. And remember, a great waiting area can also save you money in loaner cars and shuttle rides.

Make the visit to your waiting room fun! When I worked as a service manager, I held Bingo games every day at 10 a.m. and at 2 p.m. The prize? A free oil change or a complete detail. This might not sound like a big deal, but the Bingo game kept my customers entertained. They had fun, and the mood was upbeat and light. And when someone won a free oil change, they came back to my service department. The customers loved it and to be honest, my employees did too.

You don't believe me that a waiting room can actually be a customer delighter? Well, listen to this story. I read about a dentist who—get this—had video games and old-style arcade games in his waiting room. Kids were begging to get to the dentist early, just so they'd get the chance to play some games before their appointment. A kid begging to go to the dentist? What a genius this dentist was: Not only was he making a trip to the dentist fun—and keeping his clients—he was also staying on schedule by ensuring his patients came to their appointments *before* their scheduled time.

Also, who says that waiting rooms are just for waiting? Ask your customers if they might like to peruse your showroom floor or check out the sales inventory; let them know that they are free to do so and you will find them or have them paged when their vehicle is ready. Who knows? Maybe one of the sales people may make a sale! Have a vehicle sales person visit your waiting room every hour and make sure he does more than just hand out business cards. Have him talk about your dealership. Have him tell customers about your bird-dog or customer referral program, an incentive that entices your customers to bring a friend in to buy a car. Have him hand out brochures, or offer test drives, which you could call "Thrill Rides" just for fun. Make your dealership more fun than Disney World!

Be creative and figure out additional ways to make your customers' visits to your shop less burdensome and more enjoyable. Have a meeting with your employees to ask what they think would make your shop a more enjoyable place to visit. You might get some weird looks from your employees at first because most people don't equate "waiting rooms" or dealerships with "fun." But remember, it's all in the way you perceive things.

Take time to make the effort—from the drive-up appearance to how your staff promptly greets *every* potential customer to where your customers wait—to wow your customers with the service experience they will brag about! Your customers will be raving about your service department to their friends and families, and you'll have to hire new technicians to keep up with all of the service work!

~~Chapter 10~~

Opportunity Is Calling: Are You Answering?

I travel throughout the country speaking to automobile dealers, and service and general managers about marketing in the car business. Whenever I get the chance to meet with dealers in a small group or one-on-one, I'm always curious to ask them a couple of questions. The first one is: "What is your *sales* closing ratio?" Most dealers will quickly spit out the answer "25%" like a fourth-grader who has just mastered his times tables. The braggadocios of the pack will say they are closer to 30%, duly noting that their ratio is well above-average. But when it comes to school, an above-average grade is a "B". Why not aim for an "A" or even an "A+"?

You see, I like to look at that ratio from a different angle. If your closing ratio is 25-30%, then that means that 70-75% of your potential sales customers are walking away from your lot without buying a car. I like to call that your "left without buying anything ratio." 75% of your shoppers came, wasted your salesperson's time, and left without buying anything. Ouch. That closing ratio doesn't sound nearly as impressive anymore, does it? That sure seems like a lot of customers leave your lot without a new set of wheels. When you look at it that way, it doesn't seem like much to brag about, does it?

But, what really amazes me is their response to my second question: "What's your service department's *closing ratio*?" Their response is usually just as predictable. I'm usually met with a blank, deer-in-the-headlights stare. *They have no idea what I am talking about!* I had one dealer tell me his service closing ratio was 100%, which was kind of right, if you say that every customer that comes into his store for service buys something. But that wasn't where I was going. I wondered if they knew how many customers call and don't come in. That blank look tells me that most dealers have no idea how many of the potential customers who call them for service actually bring their vehicles into the shop. Do they even know how many customers made an appointment, but didn't show up? Do they know how many customers were presented with an up-sell and how many bought?

You've heard me say this before, but I can't emphasize enough that your service department is also a sales department, just like your showroom! You need to find out how successful your service department is at selling just like you do in your vehicle sales department.

One angle is to track your incoming 'opportunity' calls. Note the number of customers that set appointments compared to those that didn't, and then keep track of how many of them show up versus those that didn't. This way, you can easily assess how well your advisors are doing on the phone.

An easy way to track your *service closing ratio* is for every service advisor to keep an

"Opportunity Call Tracking Log." Think of it as kind of a checklist. Every time a potential customer calls, the service advisor fills out the log *during* the call. [Note: An Opportunity Tracking Log can be a simple sheet with five columns. Each column has the headings: Name, Vehicle, Request, FBA and Invite.] Just have them fill out the form for each call and check to see that they are doing it every day. If you make a big deal about it, it will get done. I promise.

Common Sense Service Tip #10:

At the end of the week, the Service Manager should calculate the *service appointment closing ratio* (i.e. the number of service appointments made divided by the number of calls received). This ratio will determine the success of the service department team when it comes to building a relationship with potential customers, giving those customers reasons to buy, and setting appointments (i.e., "closing the deal").

And I want you to think about this: Do you realize that about 85% of your customers will call your shop before they bring their vehicles in for service? That means they already *want* to do business with you. They don't call you to just to check on the weather; they want to do business with you and that is your opportunity. Every time your phone rings, it is an opportunity for you to make hundreds of dollars. I mean, what is your average parts and labor sales per repair order? $200? $300? More? Multiply that by the number of times your phone rings each day. All you have to do is answer the phone, be nice, give your customers reasons to come in and set an appointment.

Your potential customers are waiting for you to pick up on the other end of the line. They "took a bite" when they called your shop; now you need to reel them in. You can do this in five easy steps:

Step 1: Answer the phone! Don't have processes in your dealership that transfer customers from one department to another like they are caught up in a pinball machine and they are the ball. Ditch automated phone menu systems. They suck and everyone hates them. Don't believe me? How do you like to call places that have those nasty machines? If you're like most people, the answer has to be "not very much." Nobody likes to talk to a robot.

Common Sense Service Tip #11:

The person or persons that do answer your phones needs to be competent and trained. *Every* person who calls your service department is a potential customer and needs to be greeted warmly and professionally: "Thanks for calling Service, my name is Steven. How may I help you today?" The old line, "Smile when you are on the phone," is still true today.

If you absolutely, positively feel like you have to have a robot answering your phone, then at least make it work *for* you and not against you. Have it answer like this: "Thanks for calling (your dealership). In a minute, our live operator will be on the line to help you, but if you already know the extension of the person you are trying to reach, you can enter it now." An even better solution is to have a direct service department phone line with a process that goes to a service operator if it rings more than three times at the advisor's desk.

Common Sense Service Tip #12:

Have your service sales advisors give customers business cards with their extension on them, so when they call, customers can immediately be connected and avoid the phone game.

And that brings me to voicemail. My advice: Flush your voicemail down the commode. Turn it off. Nix it. Shut it down, right now. Did you guys get the picture, or was I too vague? I just believe that customers should get a direct line to your dealership's service department and be able to speak with a real human, really quickly. What if they are on the side of the road, broken down?

Step 2: Get Their Name and number. It's time to wow your phone customers. Once you get your customer's name, repeat it. "Nice to meet you, Joanna," is a great response. "Could I get your number first, just in case we get cut off?" is also nice. Repeat the customer's phone number to make sure that you have written it down correctly. And don't try to be cool by saying you already know it by using caller ID. Nobody likes that—it's like Big Brother is watching. This is your chance to build a relationship guys; don't waste it.

Step 3: Ask questions. "Now, how can I help you, today?" Find out why your customers are calling. Take notes. Ask questions about any problems they might be having. Show your interest in their vehicle and demonstrate genuine concern for them. Don't give your potential customers a worst-case-scenario and definitely don't blurt out high prices or unreasonable and outrageous estimates. You don't want to scare your customers away before they even come into your shop! That's just dumb.

Step 4: Be positive. FBA (*Features, Benefits, and Advantages*) should be "tattooed" on the minds of *everyone* in your shop, especially the service advisors and managers! Tell potential customers about the benefits and advantages of bringing their car in for service at your dealership. Brag about your certified technicians, genuine parts, free multi-point inspections, and warranties. Wow your customers by telling them you will check for open recalls at no charge. Give your customers real reasons to do business with you and make it hard for them to say no.

Step 5: Invite customers to your shop; *set appointments; close the deals*. All you have to do is ask. Say something like: "Let's see when I can get you in for service. I have openings today or tomorrow. Which is best for you?" This simple question will nearly always clinch the deal and get more customers into your store. If your service sales people will simply ask this one question on every call, you will increase your traffic by one to two repair orders per advisor per day, guaranteed.

Common Sense Service Tip #13:

When you get your customers to commit to an appointment time, give them a confirmation number. It can be something simple such as the service advisor's ID number. Not only does this further motivate customers to keep their appointments (customers love it), it also makes it easier to identify which advisor will be writing them up for the service.

Simply changing the way your shop answers the telephone is critical to providing a positive experience to your customers, giving them that all-important positive and professional first impression. Train your people to be polite, professional, and caring service *sales* people and they will set more appointments, close more deals, and get more customers into your drive and service bays. And that, folks, is what service is all about!

~~Chapter 11~~

Treat Every Customer Like Your Mom

Would you want your mother driving around town in a sub-par vehicle? If she were having car problems, would you give her the name of a towing company and ask her to call them herself? Would you offer to fix her car if she needed repairs, and then ask her to pay more than you told her it would be? Would you tell her to buy new tires when she doesn't need them? Would you use words and terms that she doesn't understand to talk her into buying a service she doesn't need? Would you charge her over-and-above a reasonable price for parts or labor? Of course not!

I constantly tell service advisors they should treat all of their customers like they were their mom. Think about it. When mom calls, wouldn't you answer the phone?

Wouldn't you greet her quickly when she drives into your service lane? Wouldn't you tell her exactly what she needs and take the time to explain why? And, would you send her to stand in line at your cashier window or would you handle the paperwork for her?

I think you get the picture. Many people feel like dealership service people don't care and that they are going to rip them off. It doesn't matter if they are justified in that belief or not. You can argue that one over a beer after work, but you should know one thing: Your customers are not stupid. Their perception is reality to them. Treat them with respect. They will know when you are over-charging them or trying to rip them off, and they will leave and never come back and tell as many of their friends about their bad experience as they can.

I remember a friend of mine who had recently divorced. She had gotten stopped by the police one night for having a taillight out. She didn't know much about cars, let alone how to change a taillight bulb. So, she stopped at one of those tire places.

Now, the technician there could have seen this as an opportunity to gain a new customer. He could have charged her just for the bulb and kindly shown her how to change it as a courtesy. But did he? No, he charged her for the part *plus* $20 to screw in a tiny light bulb. Do you think she went back there? No, she sure didn't; and on top of that, she told all of her friends about it. What would you have done? Would your people have seen the big picture, or would they go for the short term gig?

You see, there is good advertising and there is bad advertising. Wouldn't it be cool if my friend bragged about your store to all of her friends? And I know you know this: Bad news travels a lot faster than good news. That's just the way it is.

So what do you do if something goes wrong in the dealer-customer relationship? When I worked as a service manager, one of my customers called me after he picked up his car because he noticed a couple of lottery tickets on his dashboard were missing. He told me he had won $2.3

million in the lottery last year and that he wasn't really angry about the money or that the lottery tickets were stolen; he just wanted to let me know that we had a thief working for us. Oh man, can it get any worse?

After investigating my shop, I fired the guy that stole the tickets, but I also knew that this particular customer—even though he had won the lottery big last year and was now just playing for fun—probably went out to eat a lot and probably had found himself a lot of new friends. I just knew that the topic at the restaurant that night (with all of his newfound friends) was going to be about the thieves we employed at our dealership and I just couldn't sit by and let that happen.

I wanted to treat this customer as I do all of my customers—with respect—but I also knew I had to do something extra to make up for the negative thoughts he understandably had right then. I have always believed that if you do something wrong, you have to make it right—and I mean make it right in a big way! You have to "wow the customer" enough to make him love you again—that's just how I think it has to be done. I needed to change that bad perception that customer had about my shop into a good one and I needed to do it fast. So I immediately called a florist and ordered a bouquet, throwing in an extra $20 if they could deliver it right away that afternoon. I had my porter high-tail ten $1 lottery tickets down to that florist, and instructed the florist to arrange the tickets in little card holders like flowers in the arrangement. You see, even though I knew my customer was good-natured about the whole thing, I felt really bad about what happened, and I couldn't bear the thought of him bashing our dealership to all of his friends. Who knows how much business that conversation alone could have cost us?

I had the lottery ticket bouquet sent directly to his home that afternoon, and a few hours later, he gave me a call and said, "Wow, you didn't have to do that but, wow!" The next day, he even stopped by the dealership just to say "thank–you" in person, and get this: While he was there, he ended up buying two new cars, one for his wife and one for his sister. Wow! Did I send him the lottery tickets because I wanted something back from him? No, not in any way, shape, or form. I wanted to treat him like I would treat my mom—with respect—and to try to right a wrong; I wanted to tell the customer I was sorry and that I valued his business. I wanted to wow him and he wowed me back! Hey, I like that: Wow your customers and they will wow you back!

And, this story sure illustrates another phenomenon I truly believe in: When you do something right and good, it comes back to you. Does that mean that I do good things so I get something in return? No, not at all. The point is that you will never go wrong if you treat a customer, or anyone really, with respect. Treat *every* customer like you would treat your mom!

~~Chapter 12~~

You Had Me at 'Hello'!

I guess everybody has pet peeves, and I'm going to share with you one of mine. It's not number one on my short list of pet peeves, but it's mighty close: I hate being ignored—*especially* in a customer service environment where I am the customer. It just burns me up when I see awful, embarrassing "customer service." It's even more aggravating to me when employees who are paid on commission give bad customer service. It reminds me of the waitress who depends on tips to survive but is just too busy to acknowledge me, forgets what I ordered, and lets me run out of iced tea. Now maybe I am invisible, or maybe I am just a magnet for bad customer service, or maybe I'm just a smart ass, but I sure would like to ask that waitress what she was doing before she cut her tip in half!

I shared my "being ignored" pet peeve with a friend of mine and he quipped, "Well, Randy, they have a support group for that; it's called *everybody*!" Well put—nobody likes being ignored. Then why does it happen so much? And why do so many car dealership customer service people ignore their customers? Geez! I know I say this too much, but this really isn't rocket science: If you want your customers to have a negative impression of your service department, let them walk around and not be acknowledged. Ignore them and the next time they need service, they will return the favor—they will ignore you and go somewhere else.

If, however, you want to make every customer feel like a million damn bucks (as Letterman is fond of saying), greet them, welcome them to your store, smile, and say "Hello". From the telephone to the service drive to the waiting room, everybody—and I mean everybody—needs to acknowledge and greet customers, ask them how they are doing, see if there is anything they need, and just treat them like guests in your house, because, quite frankly, they are.

Common Sense Service Tip #14:

At least during your heavy in-rush periods, have a "triage" person out in the service drive to greet and direct customers, and to valet-park cars to keep the lane from looking like a traffic jam. Nothing is worse than having customers pull into a service drive and then back up and leave because they think you are too busy and they figure it will take too long to get service. Very often the store isn't that busy, but it appears that way and the result is that you lose customers. Not smart!

Make sure that every member of your team knows that the customer in front of them is your very special guest and that they need to be treated as such. Remind them that each customer in your shop had hundreds of other places they could go for service, but they chose *your* shop. Make sure they know that things like smiling, being nice, listening, and caring about customers are all a condition of employment—not an option. Remind everybody on your team that they need to pretend like they work at Disney World and they need to act like it every single minute of the day when it comes to customer-focus.

Common Sense Service Tip #15:

Enact the "Six-foot Rule." If any employee comes within six feet of a customer, that employee needs to speak. Ask the customer if he needs assistance. Say hi, hello, or ask how he is doing—something! Just don't let your folks walk past customers like friggin' robots!

This whole subject of being nice sounds so simple that I'm almost embarrassed to write it in this book. But in the service business, it still needs to be said, and preached and taught, and then practiced and enforced. If you change your team members' attitude towards your customer clientele from "Night of the Living Dead" to Disney World, it will have huge payoffs in WOW-ing your customers. It's common sense and it doesn't cost a dime. Just be nice, and your customers will swoon: "They had me at 'Hello'."

~~Chapter 13~~

Puttin' On the Ritz

I've already emphasized that your potential customers' first impressions of your dealership can make or break both the success of your sales and service departments, but I really think we need to talk about it some more. I really think we need to take this whole subject "up a notch". If your dealership looks like something from an Alfred Hitchcock movie, your potential customers may think twice about pulling into your service drive. You need to bring customers into your dealership, not scare them away. Start by performing a 360-degree inspection of the exterior of your building and the surrounding areas. If you can peel the paint off of your exterior walls like a bad sunburn, your lanes look like a parking lot, and weeds and trash are littering your property, maybe that's a sign your place needs a facelift.

Buying paint is one of the most cost-effective investments you can make. It's not really that expensive and that means it can be the biggest bang for your buck. *Paint covers a multitude of sins* is an old line I used to hear. Paint and your buildings will look brand new. And people always like new and improved things. It's just human nature. It's all in the packaging! Make people do a double-take when they drive by your dealership. What I'm specifically talking about is having nice, bright exteriors. You may also want to invest in some landscaping, such as trimmed trees, green grass, and flowers. I have been in some really nasty stores. They were so dirty I would feel like I should get a tetanus shot. Eww. So, paint the outside of your store, but don't stop there.

When customers pull into your dealership, they should see freshly painted, easy-to-see, easy-to-follow lanes and signs leading them right to where you want them to be.

Your service bays should have bright fresh-painted walls, ceilings, bay doors, hand-rails, and floors—everything should look nice, bright and immaculately clean. Think neat and clean...on steroids.

Now, if you take the time and effort to spruce up the exterior and interior of your place with a paint facelift, don't blow that first impression by having your work areas cluttered and in disarray. I'm talking everything from the service work bays to the service advisors' and managers' desks. Everybody needs to keep their own work areas organized and tidy. Customers should feel like they've entered a hospital operating room, not an Olan Mills studio with a million family pictures hanging everywhere.

I know I've already talked about the waiting room and your bathroom facilities and I'm no interior decorator, but make darn sure these areas look inviting and comfortable. Keep your waiting area walls freshly painted and make sure you have an attractive décor throughout. Furnish your waiting room with comfortable seating and maybe toss in a work area or two. Can you spell Wi-Fi? Even McDonald's has Wi-Fi!

And if you must have a TV, then by all means, leave the remote so customers have control over things like volume and channels. Not everybody enjoys *Judge Judy* or *Jerry Springer.*

Be sure to have someone tasked with cleaning these areas—including the bathrooms—at regular intervals throughout the day. Not only that, make a walk-through yourself at least once a day. Remember, these areas are "impression areas" where folks are forming opinions about you and your service department. I know I spoke earlier about clean, but it really is that important and a lot of managers I talk to just don't seem to think it really matters.

Now, take a look at your crew. They should be professionals and look like professionals that are well groomed and well dressed. Your techs should wear clean and pressed uniforms in good repair; your service advisors should be attired professionally so that your customers can distinguish them from just any ole "yay-whos". That's a West Virginia technical term, by the way. You don't want "yay-whos" working for you!

You may not think rolling out the red carpet and puttin' on the Ritz is worth the time and money. However, you are creating value in the minds of your customers and potential customers. When customers feel like they've gotten celebrity treatment—both inside and outside your service bays—they will better appreciate their service experience. And if they enjoy that experience, they are much more likely to return. But better yet, they'll tell their friends and you just can't put a price tag on that kind of advertisement.

~~Chapter 14~~

It's All About *Convenience*

You *absolutely must* make your service department convenient for people to do business with you. As I said before, the days of "banker hours" are long gone. Every business out there—from fast food to drugstores to grocery stores to the independent service stores, and yes, even banks!—have figured this out, and all are making themselves more convenient. Our world has changed, and you have to change with it if you want to continue to grow or stay in business at all.

Study after study has shown that the number one thing people value is their time. Therefore, if you want to have more customers, you need to recognize and respect what they value most: time! Because of this value, people choose when and where they shop for goods and services based largely on convenience. People are even willing to pay more for convenience. In other words, their time is often more important to them than their money (within reason).

Heck, I personally quit going to one of my favorite restaurants because the wait times were ridiculous. All people value their time. So what does that mean for the car service business?

It means you have to make your service department more convenient for customers. You have to be open more, not less. The last thing you want is to piss off your customers that want to do business with you because you are not open when they need you to be open, right? Think I'm off-key on that one? Go check the hours of operation for your local Walmart, Firestone, NTB, and Jiffy Lube (just to name a few). Those guys figured this convenience thing out a long time ago folks and they're stealing your customers every day (and night and weekend). You *have* to keep your doors open more to do more business and you have to make your shop more convenient to customers. Simple as that.

Now, that certainly doesn't mean that every service manager has to sign up for 90-hour work weeks and that you'll be paying your employees tons of overtime or asking them to have no life outside of work. As a matter of fact, that's *not* a good plan at all and it isn't what I am talking about. If you did that before and it didn't work, it shouldn't have been a surprise. You'd be cutting into profits and burning out your people in a hurry. And burned-out employees do not make great customer-focused employees. No, you need to staff up to be able to stay open longer. That includes assistant service managers and techs to be able to cover the extra hours. There isn't a magic formula for how many people you need, but you have to make sure that: (a) Everybody in the shop and on the service drive are working reasonable hours; and (b), your shop and service drive can turn service work around fast enough to keep customers happy.

So, how many hours a day do you have to stay open to be convenient? I'd say, at a minimum, your service department should be open all or at least most of the time when the dealership is open. Open early and close late. And you can easily find out what you need to do by comparing your hours to the independent shops in your area. If they are open all day until 8 or 9 at night, and all day on Saturday, you need to be, too. If they are open Sundays, then you need to be open, too. Hey, this isn't rocket science guys—you can't do any service business when you're closed, and if you are closed when they need you, they will go somewhere else and they just might stay there forever.

Finally I need to say this: Don't forget to advertise and inform your clientele of your new extended hours. In other words, don't let your new hours of operation be "the best kept secret in town." Being open and nobody knowing that you are open is just stupid. In fact, it's the same as being closed!

Common Sense Service Tip #16:

Always advertise how convenient you are. Put your service hours on every single type of media you use, even the sales department ads, and make a big deal about it. Convenience is the key here, and you need to let everyone know just how convenient you are.

There are other things you can do to make your shop more convenient in addition to increased hours of operation. For example, changing the way your service customers check out and pay their bill can be a big customer delighter. Please, for the love of all things dealership-holy, do not make your customers go stand in a line to pay a cashier! Cashiers, for the most part are customer serial killers—they create a bottle-neck and all they can really do is take money, piss customers off, and page service advisors to their window over your blaring loudspeaker. Wow, that sure makes for a great customer experience. What happens then? Customers tell us they are embarrassed and inconvenienced and will most likely never come back. Get rid of your cashiers. They went out with the Hula Hoop, and if you still have one living in your midst, do yourself and every customer you have a favor, and fire her right now. It will also be the best thing you ever did for your store. I promise. CSI scores will go up. Customer retention will go up. Sales and profits will go up.

Here's what I think: The service advisor—the one that answered the phone, built a relationship, enticed the customer in, wrote the customer up, called the customer and sold the service—should handle the payment process for the customer. That's just plain common sense, right? Not only will the final transaction be quicker and less burdensome to the customer, it gives the service advisor the opportunity to review the bill with the customer, explain all the services that were done and verify that the charges are correct. It's also an opportunity to set a future appointment with that customer for his next service or scheduled/recommended maintenance! Now that, guys, is a cool check out process that customers love.

Common Sense Service Tip #17:

Customers hate to stand in line at cashiers. Get rid of them and make your advisors do the cashiering. If you must have one just to make the office manager happy, keep the cashier away from the customer. Make sure that advisors actually do the cashiering as far as the customer is concerned.

Alright, here is another no-brainer for some of you, but you need to think about it: You need to focus on your parts department if you expect to deliver awesome service to your customers. It's that simple. Your parts department needs to be a fired-up, slicker-than-Slick50, parts-orderin' machine! They need to stock the parts that you use and they need to be able to get parts you don't stock—hell or high water—when you need

them. I don't care if they have to FedEx
overnight parts sometimes. You need to get
the parts you need *to the shop and on the
car,* quickly. Don't be penny-wise and
dollar-foolish. You have to have the parts to
keep the customer happy, and every minute
they are waiting they are considering going
somewhere else.

Common Sense Service Tip #18:

Don't be afraid to ask techs what they
think you should stock. Sometimes
they quit suggesting a service just
because they know your parts
department doesn't stock it. Put a dry
erase board at the parts counter, and
encourage the techs to write
suggestions on it. Review the
suggestions and see if you agree, and
stock the part they suggest if it makes
sense.

Now, at risk of sounding like I'm
speaking out of both sides of my mouth, I
will say that sheer speed is not always the
best goal in every circumstance. For

example, if your parts guys receive a part, but expedite it to the floor without bothering to open the box to inspect it, you can see how their focus on sheer speed could cost you more time—not to mention more money and customer dissatisfaction—if it's damaged or the wrong part.

Common Sense Service Tip #19:

Make it a mandatory process that all special order parts are opened and inspected when they arrive to verify that they are right. There is nothing worse than making a customer return to get a special order part installed and then finding out that it is the wrong part. Double shame on you! Customers just won't accept that kind of "lack of caring" and they will go somewhere else the next time they need service. How would *you* feel if you were a customer?

To give you another example about too much speed, I was in a dealership a while back and witnessed two oil change bays compete with one another to see who could do the job the fastest. At first blush, it was impressive as hell! Man, these guys were like Indy 500 pit crews and I could tell, it wasn't their first rodeo. But they were focused only on how quickly they could change oil. They weren't focused on performing the job right, on completing multi-point inspections correctly, or on topping off the fluids that *should all be* standard with the oil change service. You know, stuff that factory-trained techs should be doing that would set your dealership service apart from the Jiffy Lubes and Wally-marts of this world.

Common Sense Service Tip #20:

Show genuine concern for your customer's time: When a car is in your shop undergoing service work, make it a point to call customers with an update, even if the car's not done. Make that courtesy call so they don't have to call you. And for cripes sake, call your customers when their vehicle services or repairs are complete! Duh! I know it sounds stupid to even have to say this, but I bet it doesn't happen 100% of the time in your shop right now. So go inspect what you expect, ok?

Of course, I shouldn't have to say this either, but I'm going to anyway: Whatever you do, get your customers' cars fixed right the first time. Nothing ticks people off more than having to return to the dealership to get their car "re-fixed"! Put a QC process in place to check each job, and hold your techs responsible for making sure the cars are fixed right. And for cars on which they can't verify the customer complaint, have a manager and a tech drive it together to try to get the car to act up. The reason is because I have seen some techs just write NPF (no problem found) on a repair order to get it out of his stall so he could get to the next one that might pay more. I know that sounds crazy, but it is true. It's happened to me.

Hopefully, I've been able to convince you that being convenient is absolutely critical to successful car servicing. Becoming more convenient for customers to do business with you and changing negative perceptions will increase traffic in your drives and result in long-term profitability.

~~Chapter 15~~

Run Your Service Department Like a Sales Department!

*Y*ears ago, the service department of a dealership was a 'necessary evil' that a dealer had to have because the factory mandated it. They were not well equipped, well staffed, well trained, or well—anything. They didn't advertise, they weren't profitable, and they didn't focus on selling service—just fixing cars under warranty and oftentimes, they didn't even do that right.

But today is very different. Dealers need service and parts to cover the expenses (service absorption), and not only that, they depend on them to turn a profit. Car dealers can't survive any more *just* selling cars— they need to 'sell' service and parts, and they need training and traffic to get that job done.

While some of what I've talked about was geared to improving service department sales—such as answering the phone and using accepted sales protocols—much of what I've discussed earlier is geared towards increasing traffic in the drives. The latter should, of course, improve service sales; but, that isn't enough. The dealership management and service sales manager need to run the service department like a sales department. What I mean by that is everyone in the service department needs to think like the sales department does. Every opportunity needs to be maximized. Negotiate and close a deal. Don't let the customer leave without trying to identify and overcome objections, just like a sales department does.

The first thing that needs to be done is to usher in an attitude change. Hold a "come-to-Jesus-meeting" with the entire service department staff. However you present it, convey enthusiasm, and with no fuzz, how you really care about service sales. Obviously, your staff needs to know how it benefits the dealership as well as how it benefits them, too. Let your service people know that there will be goals and contests, and that their performance will be rewarded. Get the team on board. Be positive; never be negative in the way you see and say things. But, you can't stop there.

From now on, you need to practice MBWA—management by walking around. Hold three-minute sales meetings. Set goals for the day that support your weekly and monthly sales goals. Pay attention to areas of your department that need sales training and hold mini-training sessions focusing on improving the sales skills in this area or that. Show by your actions and words you *really* care about sales.

Change your service advisors from "order-takers" to *"order makers!"* Train and re-state how to best talk in FBA terms, how to listen, and how to overcome obstacles to close deals. Stress and re-stress building customer rapport and over-the-top customer service—always! Set sales goals for the service advisors—or as I like to call them, service sales people. I'm sure that you have already figured out that while the techs and parts guys are largely responsible for doing the outstanding work your shop produces that your customers should be bragging on, it is your service advisors who are building your sales and customer relationships. Let them know by your actions and words that you *really* care about sales and that you are willing to spend the time needed to train them on how you want them to sell.

And remember, you also have to train your techs how to sell. If they see something on the vehicle that the customer needs, they need to know how to convince that customer that they need it and take the time to explain why—even if it's something simple like wiper blades that don't work properly. Everybody needs to pitch in to help reach or exceed sales goals. Show by your words and actions that you *really* care about sales.

I used to do what we called a caravan in the shop. I'd pick a car that was on a lift and call all of the techs over to find things

that needed fixed on the car. For each thing
they found, I'd give them a crisp $10 bill. It
created excitement and got them thinking.
Obviously I didn't do this every day, but I
did do it about once a week, and the
excitement it created—and the additional
sales it created for the rest of the week or
month—was well worth the investment.

Common Sense Service Tip #21:

Sell Wiper Blades. I honestly believe
selling wiper blades can be one of the
best customer retention tools you
have—and you get paid when you do
it. Think about it. A customer comes
into your store for whatever service,
you charge him $300 and he leaves.
Two days later it rains and the wipers
scrub across the windshield like a
washboard. What does he think about
you and your store? He probably
wonders if you did the rest of the
service. I mean, you obviously didn't
bother to check his wipers, right? He
might not call and complain about it,
but he also may never come back.

After tires and brakes, wiper blades are considered the third most important safety item on cars. Every time you write up customers, ask when the last time they had their wipers replaced and if they say they can't remember, sell them and keep them coming back.

Create a "sales atmosphere" in the drives. Get out there yourself and greet every customer with enthusiasm and your team will follow your example. Get the team to understand what it means when you say: "Nobody walks!" Be willing to negotiate. Of course, you can't afford to give service and parts away, but a skinny deal is better than no deal at all! In other words, get your folks to understand that taking less than "sticker" for a job is better than letting that customer go to your competition for that service. Show by your actions and words that you *really* care about sales—that you have defined expectations and that you will hold your people accountable to reach your goals.

And just as important, you need to develop and utilize tools to track sales performance against your department goals—tools that *you* can use as well as tools that show every team member how they are stacking up against their teammates, and how the team is performing relative to department sales goals.

One tool you can use is a "Lost Opportunity" report. You and your staff need to track everything from incoming calls to incoming cars, tracking those opportunities that walked without a purchase or appointment. And for goodness sake, don't use it as a negative motivator by beating your people over the heads with it. (Remember: *Always* positive; never negative!) No, this report is to try to sensitize the team to be aware of "the ones that got away", and to motivate folks to strive for a perfect day when not a single opportunity is lost. Show by your words and actions that you *really* care about sales.

The best way I have ever seen to motivate service advisors and techs is to have them post their daily performance on a big dry erase board so everyone can see them. This may sound old-fashioned, but the big boards work. Put them in places where team members can see how they are performing against daily, weekly, and monthly sales goals. Put one in the shop for techs, and don't post their hours; just show on a daily basis if they are over, under, or at their goal. A simple, O = "Over", U = "Under" and A = "At" the objective will do it. And everyone except customers knows what it means. Write U's in red to raise awareness; nobody wants to be in the red!

Put the big motivator board for service advisors (service sales people) in your office and code it accordingly so customers won't know what it means. And if they do ask, tell them it is a customer satisfaction performance board or something. Track daily sales, effective labor rate, tire sales, maintenance sales, hours per repair order, CSI—whatever you want to improve—put them on the motivator board and they *will* get better, I promise.

Now, let's talk about spiffs—another motivator. I believe, just like in the vehicle sales department, you have to spiff for success. Spiffs can't be too much or too little; they can't be too often or too rare. Like Goldilocks's porridge, spiffs have to be *just right*. Hold contests. Turn up the gain in areas where you want your shop to improve. Spiffs are positive motivators for areas that need improvement—improved sales, improved turnaround times, or improved whatever. And don't forget your techs! Show by your words and actions that you *really* care about sales and that you are willing to share the wealth!

One final point: Be careful that your words and actions for motivating your team to increase sales don't get misinterpreted to the point where sales are taken too far. Let your people know that it is not acceptable to sell unnecessary service and repairs to customers in order to bolster individual or team sales performance. Explain that overselling is short-term greed and that it will kill long-term profitability. Customers aren't stupid and when they figure out they're being oversold, your drives will start drying up like a West Texas creek in July. As you practice your daily MBWA, be vigilant that your people aren't fleecing a customer.

On the other hand, make sure your people don't short-change the customer or your store either. If the customer needs or even wants some service or repair, it's your department's job to sell the service and satisfy that customer. Do you know that I've actually heard a service advisor tell a customer that he should go down the street to an independent shop because it would be cheaper? He didn't even work for me and I wanted to drop an air-hammer on his toes! And I also remember a customer that came in and asked a service advisor about a price on a piece of chrome trim for his car. The advisor told him it was just going to be so expensive that it wouldn't make sense, that he shouldn't do it. Essentially, he was telling the customer that he was an idiot. I wanted to kill this guy. If a customer asks, tell him. In fact, sell him. That is the service advisor's job. I hope these two guys don't work at your store, or do they? Maybe you should go and listen to what they are saying to your customers, ya think?

Common Sense Service Tip #22:

Get out of your office and onto the drive. That is where all of the money is made, where all of the relationships are built and where most of the problems happen. You can do your paperwork before or after the hours you are open; but, you only get one chance to interface with your customers and to see firsthand how your people are treating them.

By getting involved every day, setting goals, rewarding your team members for success, motivating people, and staying positive, positive, positive, you will increase sales while improving customer service (and retention) at the same time. It's up to you to run your service department like a sales department. It's up to you to prove to your team, day in and day out, by your words and actions that you *really do care about them and you really do care about sales!*

~~Chapter 16~~

Breakin' Up Is Hard to Do

*T*his may sound like the title of an old Neil Sedaka tune, but I hammer this theme home all the time in the car service business. What do I mean? Virtually every industry recognizes that the return on investment is much higher for keeping existing customers than for courting and getting new ones. Banks, credit card and phone companies—just to name a few— oftentimes have staffs of people dedicated to customer retention. Why? Because losing existing customers and replacing them with new ones—called "churn"—costs more up-front investment. It makes good money sense to keep the ones ya got!

So, do everything you can to wow your customers, providing outstanding customer service—all the things I've discussed in previous chapters—to keep them coming back, choosing you to provide all of their car servicing and car buying needs. That's the first thing you all need to be focused on: Not giving your existing customers any reason to "break up" with you.

In addition to outstanding customer service, your dealership needs to implement an owner loyalty or rewards club of some kind. Grocery stores, airlines, hotels, cell phone companies—practically everybody doing business—all offer customers incentives to keep their business, to reduce "churn." Customers expect it, and if you give customers what they expect, rewarding their loyalty with incentives, you'll be building solid long-term customer relationships. That's not rocket science, is it?

I'm telling you, rewarding customers and incentivizing them to return really does work. How many clubs are you a member of now? Doesn't being a member change your buying habits? If it works for you, it will work for your customers, too.

There are a lot of rewards clubs out there, but the ones that really work best are those that are simple. Reward your customers for every purchase they make in your service or parts department and let them use that reward as a discount on future purchases—vehicles, service, parts, or accessories. This is such a simple concept and yet a lot of people miss it. If you give customers good service and a real reason to come back, they will. They just will.

Every month you should stay in touch with your rewards club customers by emailing them a rewards statement that shows how much reward value they have that can be used as a discount on their next purchase. Why would they go somewhere else when you remind them they have rewards value that they can use on their next store visit? A rewards program is the icing on the cake that reminds your customers to visit your store.

You can sweeten the deal even more by giving your rewards club members priority service and extra benefits. Have a sign right on your service drive that identifies a special service lane for "members only" or offer them special discounts for service and maintenance packages. You will keep them coming back, and you will make your rewards club members feel special.

Common Sense Service Tip #23:

When customers have their car regularly serviced, let them know that you will keep *all* of the service records for their vehicle—just like their doctor keeps their medical records. Tell them they will get a trade-in bonus when they are ready to shop for their next vehicle if they keep all of the records intact and on file at your store. This is a win-win! Not only will your customers continue to get their car serviced in your shop, they will also have an incentive to buy their next vehicle from your dealership. And since a well-maintained car really is worth more, your used car department will be able to sell it quicker and for more, and that equals more gross profit. Ka-ching!

Now that you've focused your initial efforts on retaining your existing customers and reducing or eliminating "churn," it's time to step up your game and go after your next target: the customers that got away. Let's face it. Everyone loses a customer or two—or way more—for whatever reason. It's going to take a little homework on your part, but trust me, it's worth it.

There are many reasons you need to bring back your lost customers. But here are a few of them:

> 1.   You have a higher probability of bringing an old customer back than gaining a new one by advertising to John Q. Public, even if that old customer was lost because of a bad experience. A really good offer, or a sincere, "We're sorry. I hope you will give us the chance to make it right" will more often than not close the deal and bring that customer back ready to

buy. Customers that have had a bad experience that got turned around because your management team got involved, often become the most loyal. I used to joke that I wished we could make a mistake or upset every customer once just because we were so good at wow-ing them afterwards!

2.   You already have the customers' information and service records; that's a lot of information you don't have to recreate as you would for a new customer. You know who they are, where they live, what they drive, when they were in last, approximately how many miles they have on their car, and you have some idea of what they need to have done as far as maintenance.

3.   Woo back your lost customers with your superior customer service and customer focus; and remember, a "born again" customer has friends and family. And that, my friends is

advertisement that you just can't put a price on!

So, how are you going to win back those customers who, for whatever reason, broke up with you and took their service business elsewhere? For starters, go review your customer database. But, before you start calling and sending mail-outs to target customers, take the time to make sure that your data make sense. Check names and addresses, phone numbers, vehicle numbers and mileage, and service history. Nothing will ruin a well-intended effort faster than calling someone twice (duplicate records) or telling them that they're due for their 50,000-mile service when their car is only three months old. Also, check warranties and recalls—a service that customers will value and one that they just can't get at the independent shops.

After you're pretty confident you've gotten a good "lost customer" list, send a postcard or make phone contacts to alert customers about how long it's been since they were in—something you can verify with accuracy—and then offer them something you know they need at a great price!

One way to do this is to give them a great deal on an oil change—and *everyone* needs an oil change. Even old ladies know they need to have the oil changed in their car. It is the number one most requested service in the world. And everyone likes getting a good deal, so give them an offer that's too good to refuse! Find out what your local independents are charging for an oil change, *then match it or charge a little less*. You might think that you'll lose money on a $19.95 oil change—and you probably will—but once you get those customers back into your service bays and keep them there, you'll have the chance to rebuild your customer relationships and become their service provider of choice for all of their services. And besides, how much do you make when they go somewhere else? You don't have to get your calculator out for that one guys!

And let them know that this is no ordinary oil change. Sell the value of your service and remember, you aren't just selling an oil change; you are building relationships with customers and regaining their confidence in the hopes you will keep them long-term. And, when one of your multi-point inspections performed by your factory-trained technicians identifies a needed repair, who are they going to trust to make sure that the work required is done by competent people at a fair price? Why, that would be you and your shop, naturally. Are you feeling this? Are you seeing the value of a simple, discounted oil change?

Here is some more good advice about avoiding customer "churn" and for targeting lost customers with aggressive, engaging mail-outs:

- Make your direct mail colorful and inviting to customers who might otherwise toss it into the recycle bin.
- Be consistent—send the same look over and over to build brand equity.
- Offer lottery ticket-style scratch and saves for additional discounts on services to engage customers and get them to want to visit your store.

- Don't put expiration dates on your direct mail; or, if you feel like you have to put a date on it, make it way into the future—even 6 months or a year.
- When customers bring your mailer in for service, give it back to them so they can use it again. It is just another reason for them to return!
- And if you're going to advertise discounts on additional services, make sure that the offered deal is less than $99. Most customers think your prices are too expensive to begin with. Don't do anything to reinforce this belief!

So, there are some tips for reducing and eliminating your customer "churn" and for bringing old customers back to the "wow zone." As you begin to implement these and to optimize other forms of reaching out to your customers, you won't be singing *"…breakin' up is hard to do…"* anymore. Rather, you'll be taking your team out to *"Show me the money!!!"* appreciation dinners on the town. And what dealership or service manager doesn't like doing that?

~~Afterword~~

A Few Final Thoughts

*Y*ou know, I have spent the majority of my life doing something with cars or the car business: from resurrecting dead or dying jalopies to resurrecting dead or dying auto dealerships, and everything—and I do mean *everything*—in between. All along this path, I've really tried to learn all I can; I've always strived to be, as they say, a student of the game.

I've learned about cars—how they work and how to fix 'em when they don't—mainly from my dad growing up in West Virginia. I've studied the automobile industry, observed industry and market trends, and learned invaluable lessons on customer service and on how to make and keep businesses profitable. I've studied companies and the organizations from within: What makes the company do this or do that and why? But my most fascinating observations have been of people and what makes them tick: Why do they do this or do that, and what makes them do what they do when they do it. Throughout all of these studies and observations, I think I've learned a thing or two. I'm sure that through the course of your life, you feel the same way.

As I've gone through the process of writing *Why Your Customers Go Somewhere Else*, I've tried to get back to the nuts and bolts (no pun intended) of what it takes to put the *service* back into your service department. I've tried to hammer home the relationship of mutual success (or still too often, mutual failure) that exists between the sales and service departments of every automobile dealership. What I preach and teach at speaking engagements as I travel throughout the country is that *it ain't rocket science guys*! It's plain old *common sense*.

And what I've also learned from my years of observations of people and organizations is that sometimes we lose track of the simple things—the common sense things. We get all caught up in strategizing and marketing campaigns and quotas and ROIs and closing ratios and the like and we forget about the basics—the common sense things that work.

My hope is that in reading *this book*, you'll be reminded and motivated to apply these strategies in your own dealership. I am absolutely convinced that if you choose to employ this common sense approach, your dealership business will grow, thrive, and prosper.

~~Appendix A~~

Common Sense Service Tips Log

Common Sense Service Tip #1:

Once a month, get service and sales people together for a short 30-minute meeting to discuss the importance of working together. Invite service advisors to a vehicle sales meeting, and invite sales managers and sales people to a service meeting. It's good to know what the other guys are doing, to walk in the other man's shoes, you know.

Common Sense Service Tip #2:

It's common practice to take out the sales team or key salespeople to a nice dinner when they achieve or exceed a sales goal. It is not nearly as common to take out service advisors and even less common to take out the service techs (except for maybe

the holiday dinner). Fix this. Fix this now!
A few cold pizzas just won't cut it, guys!

Common Sense Service Tip #3:

Whenever a customer calls your shop and is broken down, please, for Pete's sake, make sure your service advisors know that they need to take control, take action and call the tow truck for the customer. It's called "customer service" for a reason, and a customer that is broken down needs help. This is an opportunity for your service department to shine—to be that help to a desperate customer in need, when they need it most.

Common Sense Service Tip #4:

Show customers you care by calling when they miss an appointment. It will give you a chance to get them in again. Or, at the very least, you will find out what happened to them or why they went somewhere else.

Common Sense Service Tip #5:

Be open more! Expand the times you're open for business. Staff up so you have enough people to be open, give better service, and maintain a happy workforce, which, by the way, ensures great customer service. Try being open 7 to 7. Or here's a crazy idea: Have your service department open when the rest of the dealership is open—that will throw everyone a curve ball.

Common Sense Service Tip #6:

Another great idea that doesn't cost a dime, is stapling a small brochure to each repair order that tells customers all of the great reasons they should always use your store—especially your hours.

Common Sense Service Tip #7:

Get rid of phone systems that piss customers off. Kill automated phone menus. Kill phone banks. Kill voicemail. Hire enough service advisors to man your phones. If someone calls—and the data show they usually do before bringing their car in for service—they are a potential customer. Show them you care; answer the phone, invite them in and close the deal.

Common Sense Service Tip #8:

Have a rock solid express service process in place to get customers in, do the job right, inspect the car, and get them out in 30 to 45 minutes. Convenience is the key factor today. We live in a fast-paced, 24/7/365 world, and customers just will not go where they feel like they are wasting time.

Common Sense Service Tip #9:

Make your waiting area a customer "wow" place. Offer free Wi-Fi, loaner IPads, or even a couple of arcade machines. Play games, show movies, have good books on-hand, or maybe include customer conveniences, like free manicures. Make customers *want* to visit your store. And remember, a great waiting area can also save you money in loaner cars and shuttle rides.

Common Sense Service Tip #10:

At the end of the week, the Service Manager should calculate the *service appointment closing ratio* (i.e. the number of service appointments made divided by the number of calls received). This ratio will determine the success of the service department team when it comes to building a relationship with potential customers, giving those customers reasons to buy, and setting appointments (i.e., "closing the deal").

Common Sense Service Tip #11:

The person or persons that do answer your phones needs to be competent and trained. *Every* person who calls your service department is a potential customer and needs to be greeted warmly and professionally: "Thanks for calling Service, my name is Steven. How may I help you today?" The old line, "Smile when you are on the phone," is still true today.

Common Sense Service Tip #12:

Have your service sales advisors give customers business cards with their extension on them, so when they call, customers can immediately be connected and avoid the phone game.

Common Sense Service Tip #13:

When you get your customers to commit to an appointment time, give them a confirmation number. It can be something simple such as the service advisor's ID number. Not only does this further motivate customers to keep their appointments (customers love it), it also makes it easier to identify which advisor will be writing them up for the service.

Common Sense Service Tip #14:

At least during your heavy in-rush periods, have a "triage" person out in the service drive to greet and direct customers, and to valet-park cars to keep the lane from looking like a traffic jam. Nothing is worse than having customers pull into a service drive and then back up and leave because they think you are too busy and they figure it will take too long to get service. Very often the store isn't that busy, but it appears that way and the result is that you lose customers. Not smart!

Common Sense Service Tip #15:

Enact the "Six-foot Rule." If any employee comes within six feet of a customer, that employee needs to speak. Ask the customer if he needs assistance. Say hi, hello, or ask how he is doing—something! Just don't let your folks walk past customers like friggin' robots!

Common Sense Service Tip #16:

Always advertise how convenient you are. Put your service hours on every single type of media you use, even the sales department ads, and make a big deal about it. Convenience is the key here, and you need to let everyone know just how convenient you are.

Common Sense Service Tip #17:

Customers hate to stand in line at cashiers. Get rid of them and make your advisors do the cashiering. If you must have one just to make the office manager happy, keep the cashier away from the customer. Make sure that advisors actually do the cashiering as far as the customer is concerned.

Common Sense Service Tip #18:

Don't be afraid to ask techs what they think you should stock. Sometimes they quit suggesting a service just because they know your parts department doesn't stock it. Put a dry erase board at the parts counter, and encourage the techs to write suggestions on it. Review the suggestions and see if you agree, and stock the part they suggest if it makes sense.

Common Sense Service Tip #19:

Make it a mandatory process that all special order parts are opened and inspected when they arrive to verify that they are right. There is nothing worse than making a customer return to get a special order part installed and then finding out that it is the wrong part. Double shame on you! Customers just won't accept that kind of "lack of caring" and they will go somewhere else the next time they need service. How would *you* feel if you were a customer?

Common Sense Service Tip #20:

Show genuine concern for your customer's time: When a car is in your shop undergoing service work, make it a point to call customers with an update, even if the car's not done. Make that courtesy call so they don't have to call you. And for cripes sake, call your customers when their vehicle services or repairs are complete! Duh! I know it sounds stupid to even have to say this, but I bet it doesn't happen 100% of the time in your shop right now. So go inspect what you expect, ok?

Common Sense Service Tip #21:

Sell Wiper Blades. I honestly believe selling wiper blades can be one of the best customer retention tools you have—and you get paid when you do it. Think about it. A customer comes into your store for whatever service, you charge him $300 and he leaves. Two days later it rains and the wipers scrub across the windshield like a washboard. What does he think about you and your store? He probably wonders if you did the rest of the service. I mean, you obviously didn't bother to check his wipers, right? He might not call and complain about it, but he also may never come back. After tires and brakes, wiper blades are considered the third most important safety item on cars. Every time you write up customers, ask when the last time they had their wipers replaced, and if they say they can't remember, sell them and keep them coming back.

Common Sense Service Tip #22:

Get out of your office and onto the drive. That is where all of the money is made, where all of the relationships are built and where most of the problems happen. You can do your paperwork before or after the hours you are open; but, you only get one chance to interface with your customers and to see firsthand how your people are treating them.

Common Sense Service Tip #23:

When customers have their car regularly serviced, let them know that you will keep *all* of the service records for their vehicle— just like their doctor keeps their medical records. Tell them they will get a trade-in bonus when they are ready to shop for their next vehicle if they keep all of the records intact and on file at your store. This is a win-win! Not only will your customers continue to get their car serviced in your shop, they will also have an incentive to buy their next vehicle from your dealership. And since a well-maintained car really is worth more, your used car department will be able to sell it quicker and for more, and that equals more gross profit. Ka-ching!

The Car People Marketing, Inc. Story

I wanted to share with you a little story about how my company, Car People Marketing, came into being.

After a lifetime of working in the automotive service business—as a service manager for an "indie," a dealership service & parts director, and finally, as a corporate director of service for multiple dealerships—I found myself at a crossroad. I wanted to change—no, I *needed* to change.

I realized that I wanted to be in charge of me and not be at the mercy of some corporate merger. I was willing to take a risk—and a pretty big risk at that—so I could make decisions, so I could be in charge, so I could run the show and call all of the shots. I wanted to create a business that would be fun to run, be a big help to dealers, have a culture that I agreed with and also have something I could be proud of and maybe someday pass down or sell. Oh, and I did not want to turn 65 only to look behind me and *wish* I'd only had the vision and fortitude to start my own company. I didn't want to ever have to say, "Man, I wish I had tried that!"

So, while more than a few folks thought I was crazy, in January 2001—a year's living expenses in the bank and only $3,000 in start-up capital—I left my good-paying job and started my own business: Car People Marketing.

In the beginning, it was pretty scary, I have to admit, especially when our monthly sales amounted to exactly zero for the first three and a half months. The naysayers were starting to sound smart. But one thing I've learned throughout my career is that persistence and hard work really do pay off. I had (and still have) a vision; and I believed in what we were trying to do. I wasn't about to give up, at least not until I had given it 12 solid months of good, strong effort.

Then it happened—our first sale for $5,000! It was April 20th, 2001. After 3½ months, we finally broke the ice. I often use this as an example when I talk about persistence. I mean, what if I would have called it quits on April 19th, just one day before my first sale? What if I had just said that 3½ months with no sales is enough and that I need to go and beg for my old job back? Wow, how different things would be now—lots of things. Well, for one, it's a pretty safe bet that you wouldn't be reading this book! But back to the story: May brought $29,000 in sales, and June, $52,000. We ended the year with $519,000 in annual gross sales! Things sort of took off from there.

What I had originally envisioned as a one- or at most, two-man operation has blossomed into a team of hard-working and dedicated employees, with a crack management team, motivated outside sales reps all around the country, and a state-of-the-art facility here on central Florida's beautiful east coast.

I love the car business. I love what I do and I hope you love what you do, too. Life is just too short to be miserable all of the time. So if you hate what you do, quit now and go find what you love to do. I often joke that I haven't been to work for years. Every day I get up and go to fun!

You can learn more about Car People Marketing, Inc., by going to our webpage at www.CarPeopleMarketing.com.